Gg Hh Ii Jj Kk Ll Mm

Uu Vv Ww Xx Yy Zz

Dear Parent,

The My First Steps to Reading® series is based on a teaching activity that helps children learn to recognize letters and their sounds. The use of predictable language patterns and repetition of familiar words will also help your child build a basic sight vocabulary. Your child will enjoy watching the characters in the books place imaginative objects in "letter boxes." You and your child can even create and fill your own letter box, using stuffed animals, cut-out pictures, or other objects beginning with the same letter. The things you can do together are limited only by your imagination. Learning letters will be fun—the first important step on the road to reading.

The Editors

My "l" Book

written by Jane Belk Moncure

illustrated by Colin King

Little 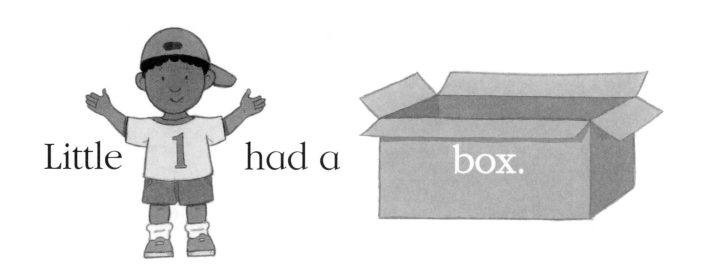 had a box.

"I will find things that begin
with my 'l' sound," he said.

"I will put them into my sound  box."

Little 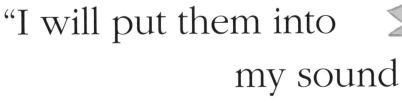 looked under the leaves and found lizards.

Did he put the leaves and the lizards into his box? He did.

Then Little  looked behind some

logs

and found lambs.

They were little lambs.

"You must be lost," said Little .

So he put the little lambs
and the logs into the box
with the leaves and the lizards.

Then Little 1 walked to a lake.

The lizards leaped out of the box.

But Little  put them back.

"I do not like leaping lizards," he said.

Little 1 looked in the lake.

Why was a lobster in the lake?

He lifted the lobster into the box . . .
carefully . . .

because the lobster had long claws.

Then Little 1 saw a lighthouse by the lake.

He went inside
the lighthouse.
The lantern
was not on.

So Little climbed up the
ladder . . .

and lit the

lantern.

"Someone may be lost," he said.

Little  heard a loud roar.

He opened the door and found a little

lion.

The little lion licked him.

The little lion sat on his lap.

He gave the lion a lollipop.

"You must be lost," he said.
"You belong in my sound box."

Little  heard another loud roar.
He opened the door

and found a little leopard.

The little leopard
licked him.

The little leopard
sat on his lap.

Little  gave the leopard a lollipop.

"You must be lost," he said.
"You belong in my box, too."

But when he put the little leopard
into the box . . .

the lobster pinched the leopard's leg.
The leopard leaped.

Then the lion leaped.

The lambs leaped,

and the lizards leaped, too.

So Little  put the lobster

into a lobster cage.

Just then, he heard another loud roar.

He opened the door and saw

a locomotive.

"Let's go for a long ride!" he said.

lobster in lobster cage

logs and ladder

leaves and lizards

leopard licking lollipop

lion and lambs

locomotive

And they did.

Can you read these words
with Little  ?

lamp

letter

light

lime

lovebirds

lace

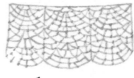

lemon

lettuce

llama

lark

lady

lock

lily

lifeguard

Aa Bb Cc Dd Ee Ff

Nn Oo Pp Qq Rr Ss Tt

My First
Steps to
READING®